DARK PSYCHOLOGY SECRETS

Master the secrets of Manipulation with Dark Psychology (First Edition)

MARK SECRET

Additionally, the information in the following pages is intended only for informational purposes and should thus be thought of as universal. As befitting its nature, it is presented without assurance regarding its prolonged validity or interim quality. Trademarks that are mentioned are done without written consent and can in no way be considered an endorsement from the trademark holder.

Table of contents

INTRODUCTION

Dark psychology: It sounds insidious, and for good reason. Dark psychology involves the acknowledgment that every person is capable of harming others, though the vast majority does not. Those who seek to harness dark psychology often have selfish, and frequently, insidious reasons for tapping into these skill sets, ranging from seeking to get specific votes or wanting to manipulate a person into giving them the relationship that they feel they want or need.

These behaviors that fall into dark psychology are often seen as amoral, sometimes illegal, and typically are considered socially unacceptable. These are covert attempts at literally controlling another person's mind, swaying their thoughts or feelings, and attempting to implant one's own thoughts into the mind of another. These skills sound intimidating for a reason—to take away one's own thoughts is to take away that very person as an individual.

One thing that many people take for granted is their ability to be free. They feel as though they are able to make their own decisions, and therefore are in control. However, this is not always the case. Consider when speaking to a child and presenting him with the illusion of choice: He may be given the option to eat peas or carrots as his dinner vegetable. The child will likely be thrilled to have been given the option and happily eat whatever he has chosen while thinking it was of his own volition. However, the child was, in essence, manipulated into eating vegetables that he likely otherwise would have rejected altogether had he not been presented with a choice. While this may seem like a harmless example, this concept applies with grown adults as well. Manipulators work to understand the mind to sway people into making decisions that they would not otherwise make, just like the child who would have likely preferred to not eat any vegetables at all. When these sorts of mind games are played on adults, it suddenly seems to be far more violating.

Within this book, you will be provided with an overview of dark psychology, as well as how to read people in order to understand how to sway those around you. You will learn about who the most common dark psychology-wielding predators are, as well as who those predators seek to target. You will be walked through several tactics used in dark psychology to control other people, including covert manipulation and dark persuasion. You will also be provided a general guide for identifying when you or someone you know is being controlled, and how to deal with controlling people and combat manipulation. This book will take you on a journey that will hopefully open your eyes to the entire hidden world of dark psychology and how it works. You will likely be shocked and amazed by some of the most innocuous ways people can be manipulated if someone decides to attempt to do so.

Chapter 1: Dark Psychology

Dark psychology is an art and a science—it seeks to manipulate others in a way that controls the other person. Through a series of behaviors such as manipulation, coercion, or persuasion, an individual seeks to get exactly what he or she wants, no matter the cost. By and large, people care about how other people feel, and endeavor to behave ethically and acceptably, but what about the minority of people who do not?

What is Dark Psychology?

Dark psychology refers to the mindset and techniques people can use to get what they want. Often aligned with the dark triad and manipulative people seeking to better themselves while harming everyone around them, dark psychology can be an effective skill to develop and master for yourself if you have to interact with other people. In fact, many people in public positions or positions of power turn to dark psychology to learn how to better get the results they want. Even salespeople frequently are taught skills that would fall within the list of dark psychology manipulation or mind control.

Keep in mind that there is manipulation, and there is an influence. Influence is normal; it involves swaying others to allow for goals to be worked toward. When influencing others, boundaries are honored and it is based on honest communication and respect for the other person, including respecting if the other person decides not to do whatever it is you would like. In contrast, manipulation is covert and coercive. The manipulator uses cunning and power to sway the other person. Rather than communicating clearly, the manipulator may lie or over-exaggerate in order to get the desired result. They may assert that they are in a position of power that they may or may not have, and they will push you to oblige them, preying on anything they can in order to get what they want. People are expendable. People's values are expendable. Anything is expendable if it means their desires are met.

Dark psychology's manipulation is primarily selfish. Every bit of manipulation is to ensure that the individual's wants come to exist. They do not care about the outcomes, or how it may impact the other person—they are only concerned with themselves.

These sorts of manipulative tactics and tendencies are encountered on a daily basis in a wide range of situations. Even television ads may inundate you with attempts to sway your perceptions of things in hopes of getting you to buy their products. In a world filled with constant attempts to manipulate you and sway your thoughts, you may be thinking, how can you possibly understand how to protect yourself from it? Or even better, how can you begin tapping into those skills to use them ethically to see the results you hope to achieve? The first step to this understands the key facets of dark psychology, from how it works to why people use it. Understanding and learning this information will prepare you understanding why.

How Dark Psychology Works

The entire construct of dark psychology and manipulation may seem difficult to understand—after all, avoiding falling for manipulation seems like an easy enough tasks to have, right? Unfortunately, manipulation can be quite covert, hiding underneath a thin veil of deniability and other pretty wrappings designed to keep the insidious nature of the manipulation undetected. There are several theories for how manipulation may go undetected, but for the purposes of this book, we will use one.

According to the psychologist, George K. Simon, there are three key aspects that make manipulation successful. These are:

- Hiding the true intentions and behaviors behind something more friendly or good-natured. The truth may be hidden behind faux concern or authority.
- Understanding the target's vulnerabilities so you can deliberately choose how to proceed. The manipulator takes the time to understand anything that can be exploited.
- Being callous enough to not feel guilty at inflicting harm to the target if doing so becomes necessary. Even if whatever is done causes physical, mental, financial, or other harm, that is acceptable.

Ultimately, the only person who matters is the manipulator, and the only goals that matter are his or her own.

Attempts at coercion and manipulation meet these three standards to be sufficiently successful to work. For example, imagine that you sell cars and you want to convince someone to buy a car that will land you a better commission. You would go through these three steps to influence your customer into buying them. First, you would likely want to disguise your interest in selling someone a specific car as concern for them. If they want to buy an older car, you may try to upsell the safety features of the newer model in hopes of convincing them to buy the more expensive car, or you may show how this newer model has some new feature that you exaggerate to make sound imperative to them. If they have children, you may try to emphasize how the trunk can be opened hands-free, or that there are a backup camera and sensors in the bumpers that will alert them in case a child were to sneak behind them.

Knowing that the parents are likely to be easily swayed by appeals to emotion, you may offhandedly mention how you had heard a story in the news about someone who accidentally ran over their child backing up, and that it was too bad that their car had not been equipped with the backup camera. You use your knowledge that parents are typically quite vulnerable when it comes to the welfare of their children and use that knowledge to your advantage.

Because you are detached from the target and motivated to sell, you do not feel any guilt about telling them the story. You *want* to instill fear in them that makes them feel like spending more money is necessary for the protection of their child's life. You want them to fear the consequences that could potentially follow if they do not do what you want. You want them to feel like their only option is to follow through with buying the car.

Ultimately, the three of those criteria combine, and you end up with the intended effect—the parents agree to buy a car out of their original price range out of fear of running over their child. You successfully took advantage of the situation, reading the situation and understanding exactly how best to proceed. These are the fundamentals of beginning to manipulate others.

Why Dark Psychology is used

Ultimately dark psychology is used to influence others into doing what you want, regardless of what the cost. You seek to advance your own interests, even if it is at the expense of another. This can be seen in a wide range of situations, from politics to television, to within relationships. It can be used to sell products that you otherwise would not consider, or sway who you vote for in an election. The knowledge of how to motivate people to do whatever they want or need enables you to manipulate them. It enables you to get the results, sometimes without the other person being aware of your influence. The most effective, and sometimes the most dangerous, forms of manipulation occur in ways that are undetected, meaning that the individual being manipulated believes that the decision how to act was determined by his or her own volition.

Manipulation in the Media

Though people often want to think of the media as unbiased or truthful, that is rarely the case. Especially on controversial subjects, the media's reports will be designed to sway the readers and catch attention. Certain facts may be omitted to sway opinions, or facts may be exaggerated or taken out of context. Stories may be meant to trigger fear in hopes that they keep your attention. Stories meant to anger may be used to draw in page views online.

Word choice is imperative, and can sway the opinions of readers, and is done to appeal to heuristics. Heuristics are ways that we understand or solve problems based on past experience. These are applied through the news. When you read the news, first, the relevant information is processed with a central part of your mind. Anything deemed irrelevant is instead processed peripherally. This information is understood through heuristics—the opinion you develop about the irrelevant information is swayed by your own heuristics.

With that in mind, it becomes easy for the media to manipulate. It may leave out facts, use buzzwords meant to trigger certain heuristics or certain opinions. If the media source is trying to cover up a story that they wish to go unnoticed, they may put out a different story to distract from it. For example, if it is a largely liberal news source and there is some controversy over a Democratic politician, the news source may instead try to distract with a story about a Republican politician doing something in hopes of distracting readers.

Manipulation in the Workplace

Workplace manipulation can be particularly harmful to wellbeing. As you may feel as though you are trapped at work due to financial constraints, even if you want to leave the job, you may be unable to. Unfortunately, some workplaces even encourage this sort of behavior, as, on the surface, it appears that the manipulator is effective. The behaviors can frequently get desired reactions from those around them, but oftentimes, that is for the wrong reasons. The manipulator may work to win your trust before slowly eroding your sense of self within the workplace and the opinions others may hold of you until you suddenly realize you have been manipulated and have few ways to fix the situation.

This manipulation may take the form of coercion or threats from higher-ups, threatening you with the loss of your job if you do not perform to certain standards, or pitting you against coworkers. Whatever the reason those around you choose to justify their behaviors, you find your own production slipping. You feel miserable and alone at work, and you no longer feel motivated to do your best. You may even feel harassed or pressured into making decisions that you do not agree with. This is exactly what the manipulator wants and in doing so, you feed right into it.

This manipulation has further layers of insidiousness— if you dare complain to HR, higher-ups, or anyone else, you automatically get identified as the troublemaker. If you try to protect yourself, you are seen as a troublemaker. You end up in a position where you comply or fail to keep your job. It becomes easier for you to comply, allowing you to keep your job and continue making money, but that comes at the cost of your sanity. This creates the false illusion of increased productivity, as everyone does work; they do as their manipulator demands, knowing they have no choice. In reality, though, health takes a toll, and over time, that health drain will drain productivity. Manipulation in the workplace is unhealthy and unwarranted, though it does happen regularly. It allows for those in power to remain there with the least amount of effort while the underlings do all the heavy lifting without risking a backlash.

Manipulation in Relationships

Healthy relationships are typically considered very give-and-take. You give to your partner, and your partner gives to you. This ensures that both people's needs are met, and you are able to create a true partnership, in which each member brings true value to the relationship. Sometimes, however, one person ends up manipulated by the other. It could start out innocently enough, with the manipulator leaning heavily on his or her partner, making the partner feel as though he or she is responsible for the manipulator's emotional state.

When one party of the relationship is manipulative, it becomes one-sided. Only the manipulator has his or her needs met, and the manipulator will slowly demand more and more from the manipulated. Eventually, the manipulated really only serves the purpose of meeting the needs of the manipulator on command. Ultimately, this degrades the relationship into an unhealthy parasitic relationship instead of the symbiotic one that most people strive to achieve.

This is problematic—the manipulated finds him or herself thoroughly stuck, and quickly begins to feel the drain and impact on mental and physical health while the manipulator only gets more extreme in his or her parasitic actions. Oftentimes, the manipulator in relationships has some deep-seated need to be validated in order to feel secure and requires his or her partner to be entirely obedient or the manipulator feels unstable and vulnerable.

Manipulation in Politics

Politics are particularly manipulative, and these manipulations can be seen with every election cycle. Consider how each party may be attempting to appeal to one specific dynamic: If a politician is seeking to earn the votes of an ultra-conservative, religious group of people, the politician's ad may highlight how the lack of religious values may degrade society. It may point to ways that people have become perverted and use that to justify how anything less than conservatism is a direct affront to religion. On the other hand, a politician looking for liberal, non-religious people's votes would likely attempt to convey that allowing religion into politics is the antithesis of what the country was founded upon and that since people have that freedom to religion, they should not find themselves under religious law. They may even point to ultra-conservative, ultra-religious countries in which certain groups of people have fewer rights as examples of what not to do, or may point that those who do not share a religion should not be forced into living a way that is religious. Both of these people seek to appeal to different people by invoking feelings of fear of what would happen if that particular politician did not receive their votes, and those feelings of fear inspire the people to vote accordingly.

The person terrified of a society that he or she may deem is corrupt and sinful will vote for the conservative leader, whereas the person afraid of being ruled religiously would vote for the liberal leader. Realistically, however, neither extreme that the voters feared would come to fruition, regardless of whoever was elected.

Political ads typically manipulate viewers through several methods in an attempt for politicians to be elected. They frequently cherry-pick details to share and neglect to share the whole story with the viewers. They seek to sway people's votes based on appealing to unconscious biases, which in turn serve to benefit the politicians, even if they may not share the same beliefs as those to whom they seek to appeal. The voters feel as though they have been given all of the information they need while the manipulative politicians only provide what paints them in the best colors, leaving the trusting voters woefully uninformed and voting in ways that they may not have necessarily voted if they had known the whole picture.

Manipulation in Sales

Sales may seem to lack manipulation, as the buyer has all the power. However, it becomes very easy for salespeople to use the information they have in front of them about you, or the information about you that you provide in order to sway your purchasing decisions. Salespeople, particularly those who sell well, are experts at profiling their clients, figuring out exactly what they want or need, and upselling as much as possible.

Some people may say that that is the nature of the salesperson's job—they are literally people who sell things. Is this really manipulative? It can be. If the salesperson is more concerned with his or her numbers and sales, then yes. By virtue of caring about his or her needs and influencing the other person with selfish needs in mind, it is manipulative. Manipulation involves influencing the other people to make decisions according to the manipulator's whims, and that can absolutely become a problem in sales-related jobs.

Consider a time in which you were a buyer, and the seller was quite amicable, flattering you constantly while discussing how there is a one-time deal right that moment, saying act now or never, and that if you do not take up the deal right then, then it is off. The deal may seem appealing at first, but upon further analysis, it may become clear that the deal is not very good at all. The reason for this pressure is to make you feel as though you have to choose, and oftentimes, people feel more inclined to give in to temptation, choosing to buy when they think they are getting a deal, even if that deal is actually misrepresented. Consider the stores that price items higher and always seem to have sales running to discount their prices. Buyers may look at these and see that they appear to be discounted, even though that discount is really just a mind trick designed to make the buyer see a larger percentage at total discount earned.

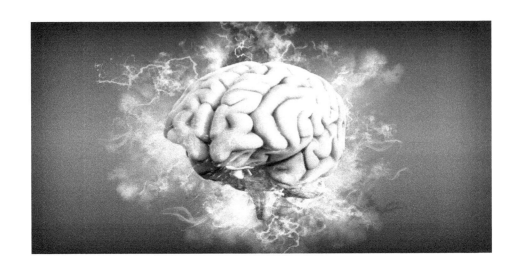

Chapter 2: Dark Psychology and the Human Mind

Body language is unconscious but can tell you so much about the person in front of you and what state of mind that person may be in at that moment. Because it can be so easy to understand how a person is feeling or what is being thought at that moment through reading body language, it is important to know.

Oftentimes, body language is broken down into the following eight categories—eyes, face proximity, mirroring, head movements, feet positioning, hand signals, and arm positions. These are the main parts of the body you should watch when trying to read someone. As you interact, you will be able to change your own actions in response to whatever the other person, and that can be invaluable when trying to influence or persuade someone to do whatever you want. Taking the time to learn to read people will open up your ability to gauge situations and how you should be reacting within them.

How to Read People

We inherently communicate with our bodies. We smile when happy, tense up when stressed, scared or angry, and cry when we are sad. These allow for moods to be communicated facilitating wordless communication. We all understand some of the more subtle signs of thoughts or feelings, such as a smile is good and crying is usually not, but there is so much more to understanding what someone's body is conveying. By learning the nuances of body language, you will have the key to the other person's mind as well. Take the time to familiarize you with the following types of body language to learn how to read others. Remember, many aspects of body language have overlapping body language, so it is important to consider the whole picture and not just a single part of what the other person is doing.

Eyes

Eyes being the windows to the soul are a trope or a reason. Your eyes, from how they look to where they are looking, can tell an awful lot about your thoughts, and many of these are unconscious and cannot be easily controlled by an individual.

- **Eye contact:** Take the time to identify whether the person you are interacting with is making eye contact with you. Avoiding eye contact can mean that the other person does not want to continue the conversation, and implies that the person is feeling uninterested, bored, or maybe even lying. It could also imply nervousness or that the person is being submissive. On the other hand, however, maintaining eye contact can convey interest, dominance, aggressiveness, or confidence.

- **Pupil dilation:** This may be difficult to read in other people, particularly if they have darker colored eyes. However, when you can identify an individual's pupils, pay attention to dilation: The dilation of a pupil can convey signs of the person's cognitive effort, and the reaction is entirely unconscious. Pupils tend to dilate when someone is interested in something or attracted to what is in front of him or her, and pupils also tend to dilate when someone is trying to think about a problem.

- **Blinking:** The rate at which people blink can also convey a lot. Those who blink more frequently are typically stressed, thinking more, or potentially lying. People who are maintaining eye contact without blinking, on the other hand, are seen as more assertive, dominant, or aggressive.

- **Line of sight:** Pay attention to where people's gazes naturally drift as well in order to understand the state of mind. Typically, individuals will glance at things they want, such as glancing at a door in order to convey that they want to leave, or looking over to a person to indicate that there is an interest in being near that person. Further, the direction one looks can also tell a lot about the individual's mental state. Looking up and to the right is typically a tell for lying behavior, whereas looking up and left implies truthfulness. This can be seen when people recite facts or describe a factual memory and their gaze drifts left whereas people creating stories or lies tend to glance over to the right.

Face

Like the eyes, the face can tell a lot about what someone is thinking. It can clue you in on emotions; whether the person believes what you are saying, and can even betray lies or dishonesty. Many of these different motions must again be taken in conjunction with other body language signs in order to give a complete picture of the person's mental state.

- **Smiles:** Genuine smiles involve the entire face. They spread to the eyes, eyebrows, and cheeks. These genuine smiles imply happiness and enjoyment. Fake smiles, however, implies that the person wants to convey pleasure, but betrays that those thoughts are not genuine. A half-smile typically conveys either uncertainty or sarcasm. Lastly, if you catch a grimace prior to a smile, lasting a split second, typically the person is trying to convey approval but is actually feeling dissatisfaction.

- **Eyebrows:** Typically taken in conjunction with eye contact and other eye cues, eyebrows can convey plenty of information at a glance. Lowered eyebrows, particularly when the person has their head lowered as well, conveys deception or wanting to hide. Lowered eyebrows with eye contact, on the other hand, can convey dominance or aggression. Raising eyebrows signifies surprise, emphasis, and attracts and invites attention. Alternatively, raising eyebrows may also indicate submissiveness or also an attraction to another person. When only a single eyebrow is raised, it may be seen as more cynical or disbelieving. When the eyebrows are pulled together, it can be seen as confusion or sadness. When the middle of eyebrows is pulled up, it conveys relief or anxiety, and in contrast, lowering the middle of eyebrows conveys frustration, anger, or concentration.

- **Lips:** Pay attention to how the person you are reading holds his or her lips. Lips held tightly or pursed typically indicate tenseness's, such as anger or stress.

Think of this as someone who is trying to keep themselves from saying something they do not mean. On the other hand, a loose, relaxed mouth is typically positive. Lips that are slightly parted indicate flirting, particularly when holding someone else's gaze, or if being used while trying to catch someone's attention, it conveys that they want to speak. Lips can be pulled back, baring teeth, which can be a smile or a snarl, conveying aggression. Puckering lips can indicate uncertainty, whereas sucking them in can convey thinking about something, or attempting to hold something back. Oftentimes, mouths will twitch almost imperceptibly in guilt, cynicism, or disbelief. Biting a lip or the inside of a cheek can imply anxiety or stress, but also can happen during lying or when censoring oneself.

- **Touching or covering the mouth:** Typically with a hand or fingers, people tend to cover their mouths when lying, as if the brain is consciously attempting to stop the lies from coming. If the listener is the one touching his or her face, it typically means the listener believes the speaker is lying. However, touching the mouth can also happen during times of stress, particularly if the fingers go into the mouth. It can show a need for reassurance, likely stemming for the comforting feelings that infants get from suckling.

Proximity

Understanding how the distance between yourself and someone else conveys thoughts can be incredibly useful. You will be able to tell how engaged or open to a conversation the person you are with is, and that can give you cues to how to continue the conversation. Likewise, you can read motions to put distance to tell you to change up your tactics to bring the person closer again. The distance between yourself and another person, particularly when intending to influence their behavior, is similar to fishing: You want to draw the other closer, but slowly in order to avoid suspicion.

- **Close together:** Someone who sits close to you is typically interested or comfortable with you. It indicates rapport, which is absolutely essential when discussing things with people, as gaining rapport means you are bettering a relationship, which also allows you more sway over that person. People may lean in when they are comfortable with someone or enjoying the presence of the other person. It can also indicate attraction for the other person.
- **Far apart:** When someone seeks distance from you, it conveys that they are not comfortable with the interaction. They may think you are lying, unpleasant, or generally, just want to emotionally distance

themselves from you. When the person actively backs up from you in the middle of a conversation, typically it is a good cue that the other person wants to end the interaction altogether. Keep in mind, however, that some cultures welcome, encourage, and expect physical distance, so this is not necessarily always accurate.

Mirroring

Mirroring is the act of mimicking the body language of someone with which you are communicating. Mirroring conveys attention and interest in the other person. Those who mirror you are typically engaged in the conversation or interested in developing rapport or a better relationship with you. You can check for mirroring by tweaking your own behaviors slightly and seeing if the other person follows. For example, take a drink of your own drink and see if the other person does the same within a few seconds. You could also cross your legs and see if the other person does the same, or try resting your head on your hand. If you notice that the other person is mimicking your own behaviors, they are either trying to build rapport with you, or they are naturally drawn into the conversation and whatever you are saying. Conversely, someone who does not follow your movements may prefer to keep a degree of separation between the two of you. They may prefer that distance, or they may be uninterested in you in general.

Head Movements

People's head movements convey a lot about their thoughts, from betraying an individual's interest in identifying who someone identifies closely with. Paying attention to how people hold their heads can provide valuable insight, particularly in group settings.

- **Nodding:** Nodding is typically used to convey that the other person is listening to the speaker. It identifies that the person has heard what is being said and that the listener is waiting for the speaker to finish up. Nodding slowly typically identifies patience and interest, welcoming you to continue speaking about the subject, whereas fast nodding implies that the other person is waiting for you to wrap up quickly. They may want a turn to speak, or may just want to be done with the conversation altogether. When slight, a head nod typically is used as a greeting, acknowledging an individual without words. Tilting

- **Tilting head:** Heads tilt for all sorts of reasons. They may tilt to the side, conveying interest in what is being said. They may tilt inward toward another individual, conveying that they are interested in that person, or they may naturally tilt toward people in power, betraying who the leader is within a group, whereas they tilt away from those who are less powerful or significant within the group. The head may tilt backward when uncertain or suspicious of what is being said. Conversely, tilting forward conveys honesty and trust, implying that the one tilting their head trusts you not to hurt them.

- **The Chin:** Consider the default position of the chin on an individual the horizontal position for the duration of this section. When the chin is lifted above horizontal, it displays superiority and arrogance; it allows for an individual to raise his height while also flashing the fragile portion of the neck in a dare for the other person to try hurting him. When positioned below the horizontal, it implies that the person is shy or sad. While a person may raise their chin to increase height, lowering is an attempt to shrink or lower height, and therefore, status. Pulling the chin back and keeping it below the horizontal line implies the individual is strongly feeling threat or judgment and that they do not trust those around them.

Feet and Legs

Considering legs are how people literally move, it should come as no surprise that they are involved in body language. Consider how we all have fight or flight instincts: The legs need to prepare accordingly to respond accordingly. Likewise, because people typically are not interested in guarding their legs or feet when trying to control body language, they rarely censor these motions. This makes them incredibly reliable when trying to understand the other person's mindset.

- **Pointing toward the speaker:** When a listener positions him or herself in a way where the feet are pointing toward the speaker, it shows that the listener is interested in the conversation. The listener is actively engaged and the speaker is welcome, and encouraged, to continue speaking. It shows good rapport and that the listener likes what the speaker has to say and trusts the words as true.

- **Pointing away from the speaker:** On the other hand, when feet are positioned away from the speaker, it conveys that the listener has lost interest or would prefer for the conversation to end. This is a cue for you to either wrap up quickly or draw the listener back in somehow. If the person's feet are pointed toward another person, it implies that the listener wants to go talk to that other person instead. The feet may also point at an exit, implying that he or she would rather leave.

- **Pointing feet up:** When standing still, if someone's feet are tipped upward, with the toes lifted off the ground and pointed upwards, contentment or excitement is conveyed. Think of someone you see standing while talking on the phone—if they have lifted their foot upward like that, they are likely enjoying the call. When implying excitement or joy, it is typically joined by smiles.

- **Jumping or bouncing motions:** Just as children do, adults sometimes bounce their legs in excitement. While an adult may not literally jump for joy, they will bounce their feet up and own. This can also convey nervousness or restlessness, so it should be taken in congruence with other signs of body language.

Hand Signals

Hands are almost harder to read than eyes simply due to dexterity. The hands have far more combinations than the eyes, and therefore, can be far more expressive than the eyes. Pay attention for the following hand and arm signals to identify the mindsets of people with whom you are interacting.

- **Touching:** Touching another with your hands is one way to convey thoughts. Full contact, involving the palm of the hand as well as fingers, implies comfort, fondness, and familiarity. When only the fingertips make contact, it implies less familiarity and fondness, or potentially even discomfort at the situation. If the touch is warm, typically, this implies that the person is at ease. However, cold hands typically imply stress or tenseness. The warmth of the touch is influenced somewhat by the environment as well, so the temperature of another's hand should be taken with a grain of salt.
- **Steepling:** This is when the palms face each other while hands are held in a praying position, but only the fingertips touch, with the palms parallel to each other. This conveys confidence in the situation, as well as being sure of him- or herself. It is a display of dominance and power.
- **Palms down:** This conveys both confidences in what the speaker is saying, as well as a sense of rigidity. Someone whose hands are downward with straight fingers seek to convey authority or dominance. The speaker is conveying that he or she refuses to change the opinion that has been made. If done with a chopping motion, the speaker is emphasizing disagreement.

- **Palms up:** Palms up and open are typically viewed positively, particularly if when paired with outstretched arms. This conveys a sense of acceptance and trustworthiness, as well as the sense that the speaker is being open and honest.
- **Hands behind back:** Typically, this pose implies confidence. Just as when exposing the neck, the individual was daring someone to try to attack, this position leaves the torso exposed. It makes the individual seem confident, powerful, and in control.
- **Hands-on hips:** While often misconstrued for unfriendliness, this is a position that conveys readiness. Occasionally, such as in the military or in law enforcement, it is used as a pose of assertiveness and used to show authority or superiority, as well as to gain control over the situation.
- **Hands in pockets:** Typically, this pose conveys unwillingness or reluctance, as well as mistrust in the speaker or person being interacted with. It is sort of closing oneself off from the other person. If the person you are interacting with takes this pose, typically, you need to earn interest and trust to continue the conversation.
- **Fists clenched:** Clenched fists imply firmness and being unwilling to give in. A person with fists clenched at the side is typically unwilling to back down, and may even be somewhat aggressive, depending on

another body language. When an individual's fists are clenched paired with the thumbs tucked inward, the person is conveying discomfort and anxiety and is attempting to cope with it.

- **Hands-on heart:** Typically, this conveys an attempt to be seen honestly. The person wants the listener to believe or accept him or her, though it does not necessarily mean that the speaker is telling the truth.
- **Pointing:** Pointing is almost always authoritative in some way, shape, or form. Think of the parent who points at their child to scold them for misbehaving. This is typically considered aggressive, disapproving, or angry. When done to a peer, it is seen as disrespectful, arrogant, and confrontational. It can be made more aggressive by jabbing instead of just pointing.
- **Rubbing hands:** This conveys anticipation for what is to come. As any sort of rubbing motion typically conveys that stress is being dissipated, it may imply that the person rubbing hands is excited and trying to relieve some of that positive stress. Similar to rubbing hands comes cracking knuckles, though this is typically done more by men than women.
- **Clasping hands:** This is an attempt at self-soothing. The person doing this is often uncomfortable at best and afraid at worst. If the hands are clasped with

fingers interwoven, it implies anxiety or frustration. The individual is attempting to prepare for the worst.

Arm Position

Arms are almost as complicated as hands to understand just because of how much they can do. While people typically try to control their arms when attempting to control their body language, the arms are still typically quite reliable when you are attempting to read someone.

- **Arms still:** When arms are still and at the side, or using one arm to hold the other, it typically conveys that the person is attempting to control their body language. This implies deceit at some level, as the individual is attempting to manipulate how he or she is coming across to those in the area.
- **Arms crossed:** Arms that are crossed typically convey defensiveness. This defensiveness may be shyness or mistrust, but whatever it is, it is enough to trigger the individual to protect all of the vital organs located in the chest. This could also be done by someone feeling awkward or unconfident, or if the listener has heard some bad news. It may be paired with putting hands onto the biceps and gripping tightly. This is a sort of way to self-soothe and typically implies extreme or excessive defensiveness

or discomfort. When defensive but wanting to be seen as relaxed, the individual may keep arms crossed while thumbs are raised upward. This is typically done when shifting from defensive to opening up somewhat. Arms can also be crossed with the body twisted somewhat, creating an asymmetrical image. This is typically done in order to show dominance or power.

- **Arms back:** When arms are pulled back, they are moved out of reach. This is a sign of defensiveness, as arms are typically easily grabbed during an attack, and doing so would make it difficult to fight back.

- **Arms reaching forward:** Arms that reach forward mean one of two things—either that you are being aggressive or offensive, or that you are reaching out for comfort. It can be an attack if it is done aggressively and suddenly, or it can be seen as affectionate if it is gentle and toward others with whom you are close.

- **Arms raised:** This is typically some sort of exaggeration, whether in joy, frustration, or confusion. It should be considered with another body language to truly identify what is being conveyed.

- **Arms expanded:** Arms can be expanded or brought inward depending on the mood. They can make you seem bigger or smaller, depending on the context of your surroundings. Extending outward conveys that you are more relaxed while bringing in your arms conveys discomfort or defensiveness.

Reasons to Read People

Ultimately, there are several reasons to read body language and people, particularly if you are interested in mastering dark psychology to use to benefit yourself. Being able to read people will be absolutely crucial if you hope to be able to influence them. After all, how would you be a very good influence if you cannot even tell if the individual with whom you are speaking is uncomfortable or annoyed?

Understanding the intentions of others

Perhaps the most basic of the reasons for understanding body language is being able to understand the intentions of those around you. You will be able to read situations better than ever if you can tell if someone is behaving aggressively or if the environment is generally relaxed at that moment. Being able to understand whether those around you are going to behave aggressively allows you to protect yourself. More practically, it can serve you well in sales—you will be able to understand whether a prospective client is interested in buying a product if you understand their intentions or whether they are receptive to the current conversation.

Boosting communication skills

Along with understanding others, you will be able to alter how you are communicating in ways that are effective in the moment. If you can read the most subtle signs of body language altering, you will be able to identify whether you need to change tactics or work on how you are wording yourself in ways that will be more conducive to effective communication in order to get what you want. Because you will see what works well and what does not, you will be able to act on that feedback in real-time. If you understand that someone is uninterested in what you are selling, you can either change the tactic or decide to move onto someone else altogether in order to avoid wasting time.

Influencing others

When you are able to read others, you understand how your behaviors and words are impacting the other person. This means that you can tweak your behaviors in real-time to develop a closer relationship with someone. Knowing when someone is losing interest, you may be able to pull them back. If you can see that someone is interested in talking, you may be able to sway him or her into trusting you through mirroring in order to develop a rapport that will be necessary at later stages of manipulation.

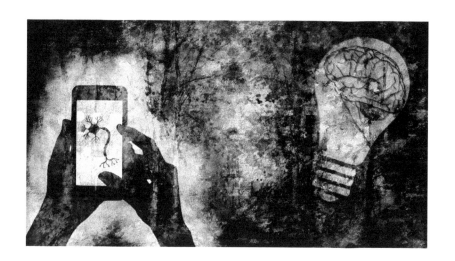

Chapter 3: Predators

Within dark psychology, it is believed that everyone has the capacity for harming or manipulating others. Dark psychology itself is the tendency to victimize others for an individual's own gain. It involves manipulating other people to get desired results, regardless of the cost to those who are unfortunate enough to fall victim to the predator. It is often deemed impractical, and in some cases, physically harmful to the other person.

Those who utilize dark psychology are typically attempting to sway other people for one reason or another, sometimes for good or justified reasons, and other times, due to extreme selfishness. Despite the wide range of reasons someone may seek to manipulate others, this section will focus on those who do it to intentionally harm other people. These predators want to achieve their goals and get whatever it is that their hearts desire at any cost, and are willing and able to do whatever it takes to be satisfied.

Users of Dark Psychology

Lawyers

In the court of law, oftentimes, juries or the judge must be convinced beyond a preponderance of a doubt of the answer as to whether someone is guilty or innocent. This, of course, can be swayed by whether evidence is presented effectively and the wording and body language used by the lawyer. While one person may say the thing that establishes the truth, another could word things just ambiguously enough that it could sway how things are understood and therefore sway how the jury or judge views the person on trial. For example, one lawyer could attempt to paint a murderer as someone worthy of sympathy, invoking images of the murderer as a loving parent, spouse, and child who has always been involved within his community and acted only in self-defense, which could potentially influence the judge to give more leniency than an alcoholic, repeat offender who is twice-divorced, a deadbeat dad, and has never been able to hold a job for longer than a week at a time. With that in mind, lawyers may also coach their clients to act in certain ways to influence the judge and jury to see them in a certain light to better the chances of a good outcome, even if that outcome is unwarranted, such as a murderer being free to walk away.

Leaders

Leaders are often either manipulative or persuasive. Good leaders act within the realm of persuasion, seeking to interact with people with an open mind and attempting to get a positive outcome for everyone involved. Manipulative leaders, on the other hand, act for their own self-interest. They rule through power and coercion, threatening those who resist certain actions or behaviors, as opposed to earning their position as a respected leader. Leaders who manipulate typically have low emotional intelligence and work through punishing bad behavior as opposed to rewarding good behavior. Leaders who rule like this are seldom successful, though people will follow out of fear. This means that they are likely not going to last in a leadership role before someone else ousts them.

Politicians

Politicians are masters at reading the cues in other people and running with them. They will present themselves in ways that come across as though they know exactly what it is they are talking about, while they may truly be clueless. They present facts confidently, using their own body language to manipulate others. They may attempt to intimidate or throw off their competition, or they may attempt to be seen as an authority figure to those listening who will have the ability to vote. They want to get the votes they are seeking in any way possible, and so they must present themselves in a way that seems confident and convincing. This is directly manipulating the people around the politician, as it seeks to selfishly influence other people for the politician's own gain.

Public Speakers

Public speakers must be able to read those in the audience, but also to convince the public to agree with them. Whether the public speaker is attempting to get a new law or initiative passed, sway your vote in an election, or even just to convince you to protest some new store, their entire purpose is to speak convincingly and influentially.

Sometimes, these public speakers will resort to all sorts of dark psychology tricks, such as using words that are intentionally ambiguous in order to misconstrue situations in their favor, or in appealing to specific groups, citing fears as reasons to not go forward with whatever plan the others may have. They will do whatever it takes to appeal to any emotional states within the audience and use those emotional states to sway and manipulate those in the audience accordingly.

Narcissists

Clinically diagnosed narcissists exhibit three key traits: They have an inflated sense of self-importance, crave constant or near-constant attention, and lack empathy for other people. Because they crave attention and want to feel validated, narcissists will often manipulate those around them to admit or believe that the narcissists are truly superior. They will create an environment that is conducive to getting what they want, whether it's from coercion or manipulation. They do not care what the cost is to the other person, so long as they get a steady stream of their desired attention and validation and the other person does not challenge them.

This is the only way the narcissist can get what he or she wants, as, without the manipulation and mind games, no one in their right minds would actually want to approach them. The adoration they crave is unwarranted and undeserved, and they cannot get it by being themselves. Instead, they must trick others into providing it. In lacking empathy, they do not feel any sort of guilt or deterrent from behaving in this manner.

Sociopaths

Sociopaths are people who do not empathize with others. Because of this, they do not feel that motivation to not harm others. While many neurotypical people naturally allow empathy to act as inhibition from harming others, the sociopath does not. This is why the average person feels guilt at manipulating while the sociopath will not.

Sociopaths are typically intelligent, charming, and also typically quite impulsive by nature of their personality disorder. These, combined with the lack of empathy, or the ability to understand how the other person is thinking or feeling, lead to someone who is prone to impulsively manipulating others in order to get whatever is desired. They may fake relationships in order to get the other person to do whatever is desired or just outright take advantage of others just because they can and they do not feel guilty about it.

Salespeople

Those who work in sales are literally paid to convince you to buy things. It should come as no surprise that they oftentimes try to manipulate potential clients into buying what they are selling. They may appeal to the client's fears or insecurities, or portray a sale as a better deal than it actually is in an attempt to sway the client into making a purchase impulsively, without taking the time to analyze or see the manipulation. The manipulation can get quite bad, with the person resorting to lies or intimidation in order to convince the client to buy, or they may make it sound as though refusing to buy will be the worst mistake of the client's life.

Traits of Users of Dark Psychology

Manipulative people are difficult to spot, in part because they are so good at covering their tracks, which is how they get what they want in the first place. Here are some of the warning signs that someone around you is a manipulator or user of dark psychology.

Dark Triad

The dark triad is a reference to three particular traits someone may have: Narcissism, Machiavellianism, and psychopathy. These three are referred to as dark due to the fact that they all have the potential to harm others. People who score highly on these three traits are typically prone to crimes, social issues, and cause problems for any organizations they may join. While all three traits are quite similar to each other, they are distinct.

- **Narcissism:** As briefly touched upon, narcissism refers to an individual who believes in self-grandiosity, lacks empathy, and is constantly seeking attention. Narcissists behave selfishly, seeking only to benefit themselves, and they have no qualms about manipulating others to get what they want.

- **Machiavellianism:** Those who score highly on Machiavellianism are typically quite cynical in the sense that they seek to further their own self-interest with no regard to morality. They typically do not see any reason to follow the principles of society, instead of believing that the only way to succeed in life is to manipulate others.

- **Psychopathy:** People who score highly on psychopathy lack empathy while also being prone to impulsive decisions and seeking thrills. They do whatever they want, regardless of the cost to other people because it is not happening to them and therefore does not matter to them. They may see someone screaming in pain and not care because they do not have the empathy programmed in their minds to cause them to care. This means those with high psychopathy levels typically go out of their way to only act in ways that are self-serving or that satisfy whatever new impulse they have.

Passive-Aggressive

Those who are covertly or overtly manipulative are frequently quite passive-aggressive. They typically rely on this sort of attitude in order to convince others to do what they want, typically by making the other person feel guilty. This is a way that they can act out sorts of micro-aggressions while still maintaining plausible deniability if anyone tries to call them out. Think of a family member who always conveniently forgets that you have a special event coming up, even if it happens to be relevant to them as well. You cannot really argue if someone says that they have forgotten about something in order to prove otherwise, since you will never be able to read another person's mind, meaning that even though you may know the truth, you have no real recourse to prove it. You are left feeling frustrated while the other person was able to hurt you through something that many people would see as harmless, and you have no way to call them out for it.

Stubborn

Because predators of all kinds are typically trying to convince or manipulate you into something, they cannot exactly admit fault or take the blame for something without admitting failure. Instead, they double down on whatever they are saying and insist that things are their way. They are unwilling to help in problem-solving, even if they are the problem, and they will adamantly refuse to compromise. Through their own stubbornness, they will double down and refuse to help with the conflict, and may instead throw more fire on it.

Infallible

Along with their stubbornness, predators typically will never willingly take responsibility for their actions, unless doing so seems to be the best possible situation. They insist that they are infallible, refusing to acknowledge anything less than perfection. They will deny misbehaviors or mistakes vehemently, and may even shift the blame to other people instead, creating scapegoats. Everyone around the predator may recognize that it was his or her transgressions that caused the problem, but the predator will do anything possible to avoid that blame.

Controlling

Predators seek control over everything. The very foundation of manipulation is controlling other people. Because they seek power and control, they will often try to make anything possible on their own terms, whether it is seeking to make a confrontation on his or her own terms, or in a location chosen by the predator. They want to keep you out of your comfort zone because it makes you easier to control. In the event that you try to get them to concede a little bit and try to make something convenient for both you and the predator, the predator is likely to insist that the meeting will take place on his terms or not at all.

Behaviors Exhibited by Predators

Just as there are a handful of traits that predators share, there are several behaviors that are particularly identifying as signs of a manipulator or predator. These behaviors all seem like they could be denied in some way, shape, or form, if other people tried to call them out, allowing for the predators to remain control of the situation as well as allowing for deniability if necessary.

Play the victim

One of the most common behaviors is that the manipulator is never at fault. They manage to twist things around so they can be the victim in the situation. Consider a situation in which a man wants to go on a date with a woman. The woman turns him down, maybe due to not feeling comfortable with the person, or she simply did not feel any attraction toward the person asking for a date. That person may try to twist things around to become the victim, saying that no girls ever want to date him because he is not rich, handsome, or successful and that girls are too materialistic and judgmental. Instead of reflecting on why someone may not want to date him, he instead turned the tables and put the woman in a bad spot. She now has to decide whether she wants to prove him wrong by taking him on a date she does not want because it truly is not about the money or fame, or to prove him right by sticking to her guns and allowing him to use that later for sympathy.

Telling distortions

Distorting the truth is another common manipulation tactic. It has many different forms, ranging from withholding crucial facts or information from the other person to making excuses that are false in order to evoke sympathy from others. They seek to use reality and the truth to their own advantage in any way, shape, or form, as that allows them to keep the power. They may hide information, or provide red herring information while also trying to skirt around the actual problem at hand and speak vaguely or ambiguously, as doing so allows for plausible deniability. If someone tries to quote them, they can say that they were misunderstood, and they actually meant the opposite. They may also say that they never said what the other person asserts, particularly if the information they were conveying was implied rather than explicitly stated.

Putting pressure on the victim

Oftentimes, manipulators will seek to put pressure on others, hoping that the pressure will cloud their thoughts during decision-making, allowing for the predator to get the desired results. This is particularly common with salespeople or business owners. They may assert that the deal has a short clock on it and that if you do not decide to accept by then, then the deal is void. The point of this is to take away time to make a logical, rational decision. Making a decision before ready can make you more susceptible to falling for tricks or takes away your chance to price-check elsewhere to see if the deal you are getting is really the best one for you. Particularly in situations involving money, you should always be wary when the pressure is laid down.

Guilt trips

Guilt trips are frequently employed to those who are particularly high on the empathy scale. They hope to push the blame onto the one being manipulated in order to motivate the other person through guilt to do something that the manipulator wants. They may assign blame that has no business being assigned, seeking to play upon the target's insecurities to coerce them into obedience. Consider someone who is willingly unemployed and needs money. Perhaps they ask you for money to buy food for their child. If you were to say no, they would then attempt to blame you for not providing for them. You may hear things such as that if their child starves to death, or gets taken away by CPS, it will be your fault. You will be told that your inaction is the reason for the problems in hopes of making you feel bad enough to cave and provide the money that is being requested.

Silent treatment

The silent treatment is a common behavior manipulative people use when trying to convey their displeasure. They deny the person the ability to voice opinions or communicate, which is immature and manipulative by nature. It essentially strips that person of his or her voice, so to speak, and leaves the other person feeling self-conscious and hurt. The manipulator often thinks that this is an assertion of power, but really, it makes it clear that they are incapable of dealing with stress and likely have low self-esteem. They may fear the silent treatment themselves and therefore see it as the ultimate punishment to other people and choose to act upon it to inflict harm. Consider a time that you may have gotten in an argument with a friend. Perhaps you voiced your discontent over something, telling your friend that you would appreciate it if a certain behavior were not repeated in the first place because it bothered you. A manipulative friend who does not care about your feelings would likely just ignore you altogether because your thoughts, feelings, and opinions on the matter are insignificant. You are left feeling belittled and disrespected while your friend sits there believing that he has managed to exert dominance over you

Lightning Source UK Ltd.
Milton Keynes UK
UKHW020638100621
385271UK00011B/649

9 781803 115146